Editor
Sarah Beatty

Editorial Project Manager
Mara Ellen Guckian

Managing Editors
Karen J. Goldfluss, M.S. Ed.
Ina Massler Levin, M. A.

Cover Artist
Denise Bauer

Illustrator
Kelly McMahon

Art Coordinator
Renée Christine Yates

Art Production Manager
Kevin Barnes

Imaging
Rosa C. See

Publisher
Mary D. Smith, M.S. Ed.

Alphabet
Cards, Games & Activities

Full-Color

Grades Pre•K-K

Author

Kim Fields

Teacher Created Resources, Inc.
6421 Industry Way
Westminster, CA 92683
www.teachercreated.com
ISBN-1-4206-8008-0
©2006 *Teacher Created Resources, Inc.*
Made in U.S.A.

Table of Contents

Table of Contents *(cont.)*

Introduction

It's never too early to prepare children for academic success! With current curriculum standards, it is imperative for children to learn alphabetic principles at an early age. *Alphabet: Cards, Games & Activities* focuses on the very beginning skills children must master to become fluent readers.

Before children can learn *phonics* (reading by putting letter sounds together to form words), they must first develop knowledge of individual letters and sounds. Each activity and game in this book is designed to reinforce *phonemic awareness* (the realization that words are composed of separate sounds and the ability to hear and manipulate those sounds). When children develop letter and sound recognition skills and practice forming and manipulating letters, they are getting ready to read.

Maximum exposure to letters is a must at this stage. Young children need frequent repetition. They have to see a letter often and learn the sound or sounds associated with that letter. Learning about letters can be presented in a fun, relaxed way. The purposeful, hands-on practice included in this book will help children improve and master essential pre-reading skills. The activities in this book enable children to see, hear, and touch while learning about the alphabet. These visual, auditory, and hands-on experiences reinforce literacy development.

In today's lively classroom, it makes sense to connect the study of letters and letter sounds with other curricular areas. Teaching the alphabet using a thematic approach helps children become familiar with the letters while singing, listening, drawing, role-playing, and creating. In this book activities and patterns related to specific letters are incorporated into most areas of the curriculum. Remember to emphasize that you are doing the thematic activity because of the beginning letter.

After introducing the first few letters, you will find that the children will look forward to the next letter and activities. Learning the ABC's has never been so much fun!

How to Use This Book

Uppercase and Lowercase Letters

The full-color uppercase and lowercase letters can be used to introduce each new letter at the beginning of a unit. The uppercase and lowercase versions of a letter can also be used on a bulletin board display to feature the letter currently being studied, or the complete set of letters can be displayed around the room to create a colorful visual reminder for the children. Enlarge the letters to give to the children, and have them use these sheets to practice outlining, tracing, and filling in the letters with a variety of materials. (See pages 6–10 for related suggestions.) Try using the letters as headings for a word wall. Children can also collect pictures of things beginning with specific letters. Set up a floor activity using the large letter cards. Suggest that children form lines behind the beginning letter of their names.

Cross-Curricular Activity Cards

Two activities for each letter connect the language arts curriculum with other subject areas such as math, science, oral language, listening skills, social studies, music, and art. These activities can be used as whole-group learning experiences, centers, pair activities, or independent practice. It takes many different teaching methods and styles to meet children's learning needs. Therefore, the cards present curricular activities while keeping in mind different intelligences: verbal/linguistic, logical/mathematical, visual/spatial, body/kinesthetic, musical, interpersonal, intrapersonal, and naturalist (Howard Gardner, 1983; 2000). The cards inform teachers of all the necessary materials and preparation, including essential information to share with the children at the beginning of the activity. The numbered directions tell the child exactly what to do to complete the activity. The curriculum focus can be determined by looking at the logo at the top of each activity card. The symbols indicate the focus for each activity, but you will find that most activities address more than one curriculum area.

 Math   **Oral Language**   **Phonemic Awareness**

 Social Studies   **Listening**   **Music**

 Science   **Art**

Student Reproducibles

At least one student reproducible is included for each letter of the alphabet. The reproducibles are designed to be used in centers, as seatwork, or for home practice. They correspond to the activity cards in a variety of formats: recording sheets, extensions, or home activities. The reproducibles provide needed documentation to represent what each child is learning, while giving him or her opportunities to share what is going on at school. Children need independent practice to reinforce the new information they learn about each letter. The student reproducibles are natural follow-ups to whole-class instruction, allowing children to acquire skills in many curricular areas.

Picture Cards

The picture cards can be used for a variety of activities. Use the picture cards during the presentation of each letter. Cards can be sorted according to beginning sound, type of picture (e.g., animal, insect, etc.) the individual letters, or as a review at the end of the year.

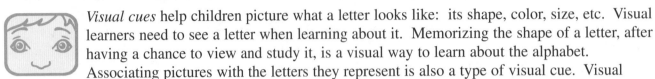

Letter/Sound Presentation

Children learn in many different ways. Some need visual cues; others prefer auditory or hands-on cues. Still others need all three styles to fully learn a new concept. The sample outline below teaches children a new letter, emphasizing visual, auditory, and hands-on cues.

Visual cues help children picture what a letter looks like: its shape, color, size, etc. Visual learners need to see a letter when learning about it. Memorizing the shape of a letter, after having a chance to view and study it, is a visual way to learn about the alphabet. Associating pictures with the letters they represent is also a type of visual cue. Visual learners practice alphabetic principles by seeing charts, lists, maps, photographs, and illustrations. Underlining a certain letter in a string of words, writing the letter several times, and tracing the letter all provide visual learners with needed practice.

Auditory cues allow children to answer the following: What does this letter say? What is this letter's name? Auditory learners need to frequently hear a letter name and the sound or sounds associated with it. They also enjoy repeatedly saying the letter name and sound(s). Saying words that start with a particular letter reinforces phonemic awareness for an auditory learner. Memorizing a list of objects that start with a certain sound can increase their skills, too. Saying a letter name and sound(s) while looking at corresponding picture cards is another productive activity. An auditory learner enjoys talking about what he or she is learning. He or she likes to listen to stories, focusing on the tone, pitch, and speed of the person's voice. Music, class discussions, and group brainstorming activities are perfect for auditory learners.

Hands-on cues enable children to use their sense of touch, while using their hands and fingers, to learn about the alphabet. When a hands-on (sensory/tactile) learner has opportunities to feel the shape, size, and texture of a letter, he or she develops an understanding of the alphabet. Hands-on learners love to use their bodies to accomplish a learning task: forming letters with their bodies (individually or with a partner), acting out the meaning of a word, or touching letters in a variety of textures. A hands-on learner discovers new things through movement and exploration of the environment, preferring interaction rather than watching, listening, or reading. He or she loves to put things together and create new things. A hands-on learner enjoys participating in kinesthetic activities such as action games, finger plays, charades, card games, skits, pantomimes, role-plays, experiments, and demonstrations.

The following ideas can be used with every letter of the alphabet. Allow the children to complete a variety of activities for each letter. Repeat the activities that are popular with the children. Use the activities on this page and pages 7–10 as a springboard to create even more ways to practice the alphabet!

Sample Presentation of a Letter

The following outline can be used each time you introduce a new letter to the children:

1. Take a close look at the uppercase or lowercase letter. What does the letter look like (e.g., *O* looks like a circle)? Talk about the lines, curves, etc.
2. Memorize the shape of the letter.
3. Practice writing the letter in the air, accentuating the lines and curves.
4. Say the sound the letter makes.
5. Say a word (show a picture card for that letter) that starts with that sound.
6. Name other words that start with the same sound.
7. List names of children in the class that start with this letter.

Activities for Every Letter

Forming the Shape of a Letter

Children need lots of practice forming letters on many different textures, surfaces, and media. This is a good activity for visual and hands-on learners to complete. Children can practice forming each letter, using their fingers to manipulate the following materials:

- sand in a sandbox
- shaving cream
- rice in a tray
- pudding in a dish
- cooked spaghetti
- Wikki® Sticks
- play dough
- paint inside a clear, resealable plastic bag

Outlining a Letter

Children can practice tracing around a copy of the letter. This is very helpful for hands-on and visual learners. To outline a letter, children can use the following:

- crayons to do a rainbow-outline
- glue
- squeeze glitter
- toothbrush dipped in paint
- marshmallow dipped in ink
- beans
- small beads
- pasta

Tracing a Letter

Children can practice tracing over a copy of the letter. Visual and hands-on learners will enjoy these activities. To trace a letter, children can do the following:

- use cinnamon sticks to trace a sandpaper, cutout version of the letter
- use a cotton swab dipped in water to trace a copy of the letter
- use a paintbrush with paint to trace a construction-paper copy of the letter

Writing a Letter

Writing is another way for visual and hands-on learners to learn about a letter. Children can use many different writing instruments to practice writing letters. Varying the instruments and surfaces on which children write provides an assortment of tactile experiences. Children can practice writing a letter using a variety of instruments (e.g., gel pens, colored pencils, markers, chalk, erasable marker) and/or a variety of writing surfaces (e.g., chalkboard, white board, sandpaper).

For an alternative, place pieces of paper on top of a variety of objects (e.g., sandpaper, carpet, pillow) and have children draw on the paper using one of the instruments listed above.

Outside, supply a variety of different sizes and styles of paintbrushes and buckets of water. Encourage children to write (paint) on paper placed against walls, doors, and pavement. (Keep safety issues in mind when children participate in this activity.)

Activities for Every Letter *(cont.)*

Filling in a Letter

Children can better understand the shape of a letter when they are allowed to fill it with many different objects. This is especially good for visual and hands-on learners. To fill in a letter, children can use the following:

- torn tissue paper
- stamps and ink pad
- dots (pencil-eraser stamp)
- dropper filled with colored water

- pictures in letters (apple in the letter A)
- pictures of objects (collage)
- object that starts with a certain letter (popcorn or paper for the letter P)

Using Manipulatives to Create a Letter

Manipulatives work especially well for hands-on learners. Children learn as they touch and feel different textures. Try the following suggestions to create letters:

- lacing cards—First, copy full-color letter pages onto tagboard and laminate. Punch evenly-spaced holes about 1" (2.5 cm) apart, around the entire edge of the letter. Finally tie a colorful shoelace to one of the holes and have a child use the shoestring to "sew" around the letter.

- puzzle pieces—Cut apart a full-color letter page; student puts puzzle pieces together to form a letter.

- pegs on a pegboard

- shape letters using dough—cookie, pretzel or playdough.

Playdough Recipe

- 4 cups of water
- small bottle of food coloring
- 4 tablespoons vegetable oil

- 4 cups flour
- 2 cups salt
- 1.5 oz. Cream of Tartar

optional: scented oil (lavendar, pine, orange, or almond oil work well)

1. Combine the liquid ingredients (water, food coloring, oil, scent) in a pot and bring to a boil.
2. Combine the dry ingredients (flour, salt, Cream of Tartar) in a large mixing bowl.
3. Pour the liquid mixture into the dry ingredients and blend until smooth.
4. Let the mixture cool and knead the dough to the desired consistency.

Activities for Every Letter (cont.)

Oral Activities

The following activities work well for auditory learners.

- Name a child in your class and have the children suggest something that this person likes that starts with the same letter (i.e., Anna likes apples, Bobby likes bears).

- Share a morning message with the children that has several words starting with the same letter (e.g., *Today* is *Tuesday*. We will learn how to *tie* a bow.). Have the children tell you the words they heard that start with a certain letter.

- Read a tongue twister to children. Have the children repeat aloud with you *only* the words that start with the same sound.

Combination Activities

The activities in this category incorporate a variety of learning styles: visual, auditory, and hands-on.

- Walk around the room to find a certain letter in words. Use the full-color "letter finder" patterns on pages 11 and 13. Cut out the retangle in each pattern. Use this "window" to find letters in the room. Or purchase inexpensive fly swatters and cut out holes from the middle.

- While sharing a Big Book, have the children clap, wiggle, etc., any time they see a word starting with a certain letter.

- Place a sticker or small picture on each child's index finger. Allow the children to play with the "finger puppet" for a few minutes. Review the letter that the puppet represents (i.e., a parrot puppet for the letter *p*). As a class, brainstorm words that start with that letter (e.g., popcorn, pudding, pet, park). Write a sentence that includes several of the brainstormed words (e.g., My **p**urple **p**et **p**arrot likes to eat **p**ink **p**opcorn.). Read the sentence aloud. Have the children repeat the sentence with you.

- Have the children bring objects that start with a certain letter to share with the class.

Ideas for Using More Than One Letter

- Place 12 picture cards (four cards representing three different letters, e.g., D, E, F) on a table. Have children match each picture to its corresponding letter.

- In a sentence, have the children underline a certain letter, circle another letter, etc.

The c(a)t s(a)t on my l(a)p.

- Have the children count how many times a certain letter appears in a sentence.

- Share with the children an alliterative book, such as *Animalia* by Graeme Base (Harry N. Abrams, 1987). Use a pointer to show the repeated letter on each page (e.g., On the *A* page, point out each *a*: "An armoured armadillo avoiding an angry alligator").

- Using six full-color letter cards (e.g., *A, a, B, b, C, c*), match each uppercase letter to its corresponding lowercase version.

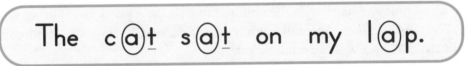

- Use magnetic letters to attach corresponding picture cards to a magnetic board.

- Hang a letter card with its corresponding picture cards on a clothesline.

- Sort picture cards into cups labeled with letters.

- Sort six picture cards using the following game: "Bobby likes _____." Only give Bobby the picture cards that start with the letter *b*. Bobby does not like the picture cards that start with letters other than *b*. (Use the names of children in your class to complete this activity.)

- Create or purchase an Alphabet Bingo game to play during group time.

Letter Finders

Letter Finders

A Is for Ant

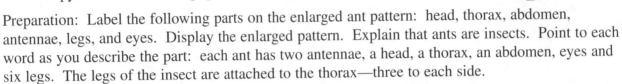

Materials

- 1 enlarged copy of Ant Pattern (page 18)
- 1 copy of Ant Pattern (page 18) for each child
- 1 copy of Find the Ants (page 19) for each child

Preparation: Label the following parts on the enlarged ant pattern: head, thorax, abdomen, antennae, legs, and eyes. Display the enlarged pattern. Explain that ants are insects. Point to each word as you describe the part: each ant has two antennae, a head, a thorax, an abdomen, eyes and six legs. The legs of the insect are attached to the thorax—three to each side.

Objective: Children will learn how to identify insect body parts using this science activity.

Directions

1. Using the enlarged ant pattern, have a child locate the ant's head. Have another child tell about the parts on the head (*two antennae, two eyes*).
2. Point out the ant's thorax. Have the children pronounce the word *thorax* a few times. Have a volunteer point to each of the ant's six legs. Note the way they are arranged in pairs.
3. Ask another volunteer to tell the name of the last part (*abdomen*). Have the children pronounce the word *abdomen* several times. Review each part of the ant while you point to it.
4. Provide each child with a copy of Find the Ants as an extension activity. Instruct each child to remember what he or she has learned about ants and to only circle the ants in the picture.
5. Give each child a copy of Ant Pattern. Have them complete the labeling assignment at home and talk about the parts of an ant with a family member.

A Is for Apple

Materials

- 1 basket
- 2 red apples; 3 yellow apples; 4 green apples
- 1 copy of How Many Apples? (page 20) for each child

Preparation: Place the red, yellow and green apples in a basket at a center. Discuss that apples come in different colors. Practice counting from 1–10 as a group. Give each student a copy of How Many Apples?

Objective: Students will use apples to practice counting skills at this math center.

Directions

1. Count the red apples in the basket. Color the matching number of apples red.
2. Count the green apples in the basket. Color the matching number of apples green.
3. Count the yellow apples in the basket. Color the matching number of apples yellow.
4. Count all the apples. Circle the total number of apples.

Name _____

A Is for Ant

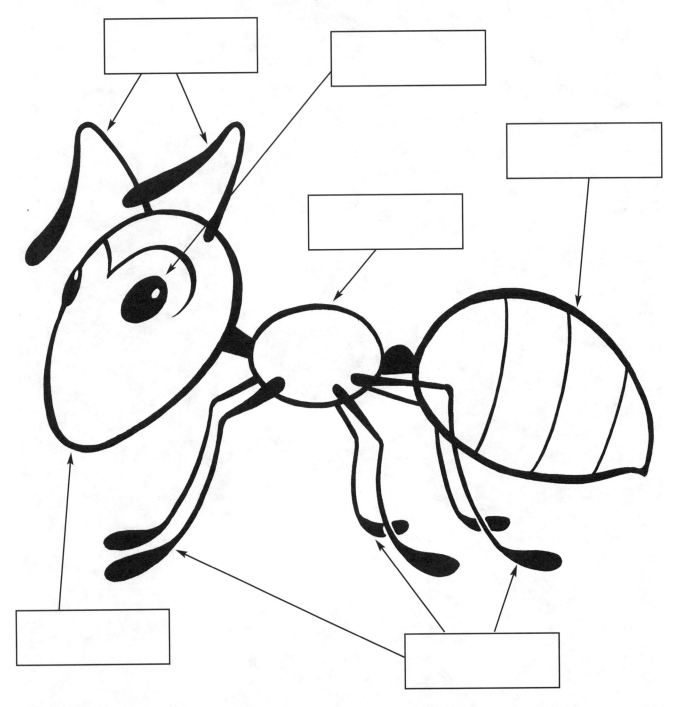

Directions: Cut out the word labels. Use them to label the ant's body parts.

antennae	legs	thorax
abdomen	head	eyes

Find the Ants

I found ☐ ants.

Directions: Circle the ants on the page. How many ants did you find?

Name _____

How Many Apples?

1 2 3 4 5 6 7 8 9 10

Directions

- Count the *red* apples. Color the matching number of apples red.
- Count the *green* apples. Color the matching number of apples green.
- Count the *yellow* apples. Color the matching number of apples yellow.
- Count *all* the apples. Circle the total number of apples.

Aa

apple Aa

alligator   ant

B Is for Baby

Materials

- 1 small blanket (baby blanket or small towel)
- 3 baby items that start with *b*, and two baby items that do not start with b.
- 1 enlarged copy of Baby Items (page 26)

Objective: Students will review words/items that start with *b* using this center activity.

Directions

1. Tell the children that you will be talking about things that start with the letter *b*. Say /b/ and have the children repeat the sound.

2. Show the children the baby items. Have volunteers name each object. As a class, sort the items into two piles: those that start with *b* and those that do not.

3. Discuss things that are associated with babies (e.g., stroller, high chair, crib, ball). Point out that *ball* starts with the same letter as *baby*.

4. At a center, have the children sort the baby items into two groups: those items that start with *b* and those items that do not. Have the children place each baby item that starts with *b* on the baby blanket. Later, have students do the Baby Items worksheet.

B Is for Bear

Materials

- large teddy bear

Objective: Children will apply the abstract concept of pairs in this hands-on activity.

Directions

1. Explain that a *pair* is "two similar things."

2. Have the children look at the teddy bear. Point out that the bear has two eyes, or a *pair* of eyes.

3. Have volunteers come to the bear and show another pair (e.g., ears, legs, feet, arms, paws).

4. Allow the children time to find pairs on their own bodies. Then invite volunteers to share those pairs with the class.

Baby Items

Directions: Color and cut out each baby item. Sort the items into two piles: those that start with *b*, and those that do not. Put only the items that start with *b* on the blanket.

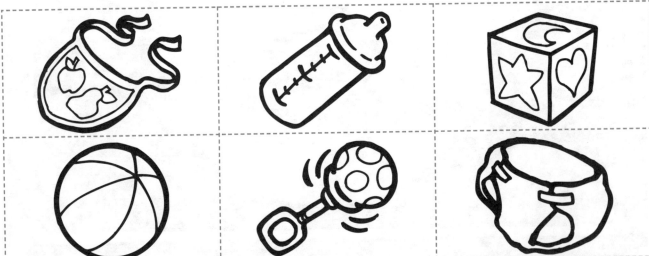

Bb

bears **Bb**

bow banana

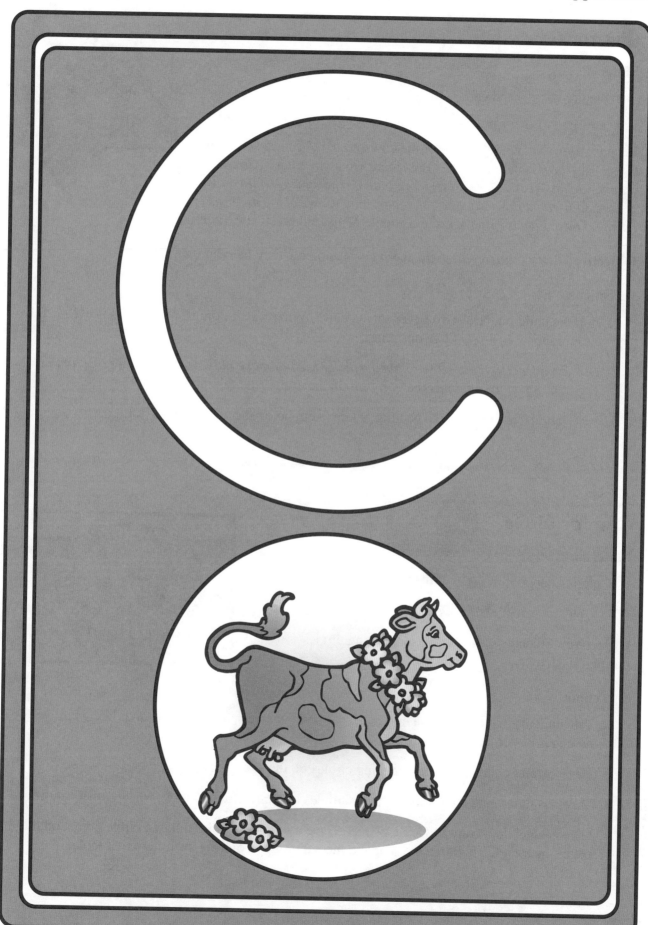

C Is for Cow

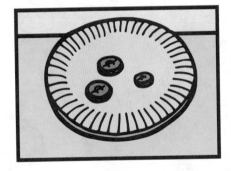

Materials

- picture of cow and calf
- a variety of dairy products (e.g., milk, yogurt, or butter carton)

Preparation: Show the picture of the cow and calf. Tell the children that a baby cow is called a calf. Talk about what cows eat. (*Cows eat plants, such as grass. A cow has more than one stomach, so it can eat grass and break it down to digest the nutrients. Cows also eat corn, hay, and mixed feeds* [grains, protein supplements, minerals, and vitamins]).

Objective: The children will learn about cows and how they help humans.

Directions

1. Ask the children, "Have you ever seen a cow? What was it doing? Where did it live?" Tell children that most cows live on farms.

2. Discuss how cows help us (*e.g., their milk is used to make milk to drink, cheese, butter, and yogurt*). Show the students the dairy product cartons, and talk about what they are.

3. Ask volunteers to take turns naming a dairy item he or she ate for breakfast.

C Is for Circle

Materials

- circle-shaped items (e.g., hula hoop, coin, paper plate)
- 1 copy of Circle Scene (page 32) for each child

Objective: Students will practice identifying circles during this activity.

Directions

1. Tell students that a *circle* is a curved shape without lines. A circle is round, like a ball with no edges or corners.

2. Have several children practice making circles on the chalkboard.

3. Take a walk around the room to find examples of a circle (e.g., clock, wheel, trash can rim).

4. Give each child a copy of Circle Scene. Have a volunteer point out one circle object on the page. Instruct the children to complete the activity by coloring each item that looks like a circle.

Name _____

Circle Scene

I found ☐ circles.

- -

Directions: Color each item that looks like a circle.

Cc

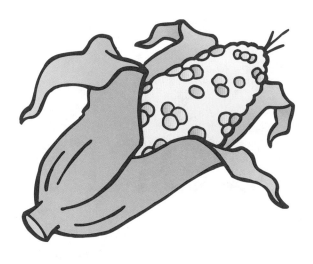

cow Cc

cat corn

D Is for Dinosaur

Materials

- centimeter cubes (Unifix®)
- 1 copy of Measure the Dinosaurs (page 38) for each child

Objective: Children will learn how to use non-standard measurement tools to measure objects.

Directions

1. Using centimeter cubes, show the children how to measure a crayon. Place the crayon on a flat surface. Start at the bottom, stacking the cubes on top of each other. Stop stacking the cubes when they get to the top of the crayon. Count the cubes.
2. Using the same method, show how to measure the length of a sheet of paper.
3. Ask a volunteer to show how to measure the height of one of the dinosaurs on Measure the Dinosaurs.
4. At a center, have each child use the centimeter cubes to measure each dinosaur and record the number of cubes in the corresponding box.

D Is for Dog

Materials

- oats
- 1 sheet of art paper for each child
- different colors of yarn cut into smaller pieces
- coffee grounds

Objective: Students will use different shapes to create a drawing.

Directions

1. Talk about dogs. What type of covering do they have? (*fur*) Have a few volunteers tell what fur feels like. (*soft, smooth, fuzzy*)
2. Give each child a sheet of paper. Demonstrate how to draw a simple dog, one step at a time.
3. Draw a long oval, lengthwise (dog's body).
4. Draw 1 large circle (head).
5. Draw 2 ovals (ears).
6. Draw 2 small circles (eyes) and 1 small triangle (nose).
7. Draw 4 short, skinny ovals (legs) below the body.
8. Draw 4 small circles (paws) at the ends of the legs.
9. Add a long, skinny oval (tail) and a mouth to the dog.
10. Attach oats, yarn, or coffee grounds to your dog to create the fur.

Name _____

Measure the Dinosaurs

Directions: Using centimeter cubes, measure how tall each dinosaur is. Write the number in the box by the dinosaur. Circle the tallest dinosaur.

Dd

dog Dd

deer dance

E Is for Egg

Materials

- play dough
- pictures of a hummingbird, a chicken, and an ostrich

Preparation: Use the play dough to form eggs in 3 different sizes (pea-shaped, chicken egg, and ostrich egg 5 in. diameter x 6 in. long).

Objective: Introduce your students to the incredible world of science through this hands-on egg activity. Students will match eggs to corresponding birds.

Directions

1. Show the pictures of the ostrich, chicken, and hummingbird.

2. Tell students that each bird lays eggs. Ask the children to tell you which bird lays the biggest egg? smallest egg?

3. Pass around the three eggs so that each child can feel them.

4. Have volunteers match each egg to the picture of the corresponding bird.

E Is for Elf

Materials

- elf doll (or other small doll)
- 1 copy of Elves Are Everywhere! (page 44) for each child

Objective: Children will learn about prepositions (spatial concepts) using this fun listening activity.

Directions

1. Review with children vocabulary that deals with location (e.g., on, under, above, below, beside).

2. Have several children use the elf doll to show a variety of commands (e.g., Place the elf on the table.).

3. Give each child a copy of Elves Are Everywhere! Tell students that they must listen carefully to complete this activity.

4. Read aloud the first direction and have a volunteer show the class how to complete it.

5. Have each child complete the activity independently as you read aloud the remaining directions.

42

Name _____

Elves Are Everywhere!

Directions

1. Circle the elf *under* the tree.

2. Color the elf *beside* the flower blue.

3. Color the elf *above* the jump rope red.

4. Cross out the elf *on* the swing.

Ee

elephant **Ee**

elf egg

F Is for Frog

Materials

- frog thumbprints
- brown or green paint or inkpad
- 1 sheet of white construction paper for each child

Preparation: Make a few frog thumbprints (see sample on this page) to display for students.

Objective: Students will use their fingers *and* their imaginations to create frog thumbprints.

Directions

1. Show children how to make a thumbprint using paint or inkpad on construction paper.
2. Demonstrate how to turn the thumbprint into a simple frog using a pencil to draw the eyes, mouth, ears, and legs.
3. Show what happens when using other fingers for prints, especially by comparing sizes and shapes of the thumb and pinkie finger.
4. Display the large frog thumbprints at a center. Each child uses his or her finger, paint, and a pencil or crayons to make a frog thumbprint on a sheet of paper. Encourage each child to make several frogs using different fingers.
5. Have each child select his or her favorite frog. Have the student write his or her name, with assistance as needed. Cut out the frog thumbprints and display them on a bulletin board titled "Look at Our Frogs!"

F Is for Friend

Materials

- 1 copy of My Friend (page 50) for each child

Objective: Each child can build interpersonal skills while conducting a "friendly" interview.

Directions

1. Ask the students what a friend is. Emphasize that we can all be friends, and that as we know more about people, it helps us understand them and be a good friend to them.
2. Tell students that they will be asking one other child in the class the following questions: "What is your favorite color? How do you get to school? What is your favorite animal? What do you like to do at school?" The child that is interviewing will write the friend's name at the top of the page (assist as needed) and color in the best answer to each question. Then the pair will trade places and give the other friend an opportunity to ask the questions.
3. Divide the class into pairs. Give each pair two copies of My Friend.
4. Have the students in each pair complete the activity as described above.
5. Allow several volunteers to share information about their friends with the class, using the activity sheets as needed.

Name _____

My Friend

What is your favorite color?

How do you get to school?

What do you like to do at school?

What is your favorite animal?

- -

Directions: Ask your friend each question. Color the best answer.

Ff

frog

Ff

fish

fan

G Is for Giraffe

Materials

- none

Preparation: Discuss giraffes. Explain to the children that the giraffe is the tallest of all land animals. Giraffes live in groups of up to 20. Giraffes have great eyesight and use their long necks to see over trees to help know when they need to run away from enemies. Discuss the giraffe's tongue. It is black. It uses its tongue to grab leaves and pull them to its mouth to eat. To drink, the giraffe must spread its legs apart to reach the ground with the head. A giraffe moves and plays by galloping around, kicking swiftly, and running for short distances.

Objective: Students will learn fascinating facts while moving like giraffes.

Directions

Have students pretend to be giraffes by doing the following movements:

1. Use their long necks to crane over trees looking for lions.

2. Use their tongues to pretend to grab leaves off trees.

3. Drink water by spreading their legs apart and reaching down for the ground with their heads.

4. Play like a baby giraffe: run, kick, and gallop!

G Is for Goose

Materials

- Copy of Goose Puppets (page 56) for the teacher

- 1 copy of Goose Puppets (page 56) for each child

- 1 copy of "One Little Goose" (page 56) for each child

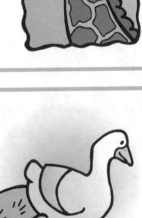

Preparation: Color, cut out, and assemble the Goose Puppets.

Objective: Students practice storytelling skills using finger puppets.

Directions

1. Read aloud to children "One Little Goose" several times. (*Note: The version is modified from the traditional poem, "This Little Piggy."*)

2. Show the children how to use each finger puppet with its corresponding line.

3. Have students take home a copy of Goose Puppets and "One Little Goose." A family member can help the child assemble the finger puppets and read aloud the poem, while the child moves the correct finger puppet. Then have the child retell the poem, line by line, using the finger puppets.

Goose Puppets

One Little Goose

One little goose swims quickly.

One little goose stays dry.

One little goose eats pond plants.

One little goose flies high.

One little goose cries
"Honk, honk, honk,"
all the day long.

Honk, Honk, Honk!

Directions: Color and cut out the finger puppets. Roll the base of each puppet to fit and tape it into position. Recite "One Little Goose" while your child uses the puppets to act out the rhyme. Encourage your child to retell the poem using the finger puppets.

Gg

goose Gg

glue glove

59

H Is for Helper

Materials

- 1 copy of Community Helper Letter (page 62) for each child

Objective: Children can present these special thank-you notes to their favorite community helpers!

Directions

1. Talk about community helpers (e.g., doctor, nurse, veterinarian, lifeguard, police officer, firefighter). Ask students how each person helps make the community a better place.

2. Ask each child to choose a favorite helper. Give him or her the Community Helper Letter to complete by following the directions on the sheet.

3. Invite each child to present the letter to a favorite community helper!

H Is for Hand

Materials

- posterboard
- squares of a variety of textures (e.g., sandpaper, fake fur, flannel, silk)

Preparation: Attach the texture squares to the posterboard and display it at a center.

Objective: Students will feel a variety of textures and describe them.

Directions

1. Talk about using your fingers to feel the textures of a variety of objects. Use vocabulary such as *soft, rough, smooth, bumpy, scaly,* and *furry*. Have volunteers give examples of each type of texture.

2. At a center, have students feel the texture squares one at a time. Have them choose their favorite texture and explain their choice.

3. As a class, have several students take turns describing their favorite texture. Have the other students guess which square it is.

Community Helper Letter

Dear Helper,

Thank you for all you do.

You help our community.

You are important to me!

_____
Name

Directions: Color the pictures on the letter. Sign your name at the bottom. Give the completed letter to a community helper to say thanks!

Hh

horse Hh

hearts hat

I Is for Ice

Materials

- 1 one-ounce (30 mL) cup for each child
- 1 small dish for each child

Preparation: Fill the cups with water and place them on a tray. Put the cups in a freezer to form an ice cube for each student.

Objective: Students will watch solid transform to liquid right before their eyes!

Directions

1. Have students share experiences they have had with ice.
2. Give each student an ice cube on a dish and have him or her play with the ice to see what happens.
3. Encourage students to hold, touch, and breathe on the ice cubes.
4. As a class, talk about what happened to the ice. Tell students that the heat from their hands helped change the ice (a solid) to water (a liquid).
5. If possible, have students take ice cups outside after hands-on explorations. Have them observe what happens to the ice when placed in the sun and shade.

I Is for Iguana

Materials

- green construction paper or tissue paper(several sheets for each child)
- 1 copy of Iguana Pattern (page 68) for each child

Preparation: Photocopy the Iguana Pattern onto green construction paper (One for each child). Tell the children that the iguana has a long tail; in fact, the tail can make up about half of its body length! Its skin is rough and it has pointy scales on the back. The iguana is a reptile. It eats mostly leaves and fruit. Some iguanas are kept as pets.

Objective: Students will learn about reptiles. (Emphasize the texture of the iguana's skin.)

Directions

1. Give each child several sheets of green construction paper. Have him or her tear the sheets into small pieces.
2. Distribute copies of Iguana Pattern to the students. Have each child glue the torn-paper pieces on the iguana for the scales.
3. Allow the children to take home their iguana pictures and tell their families neat facts about the iguana.

Name _____

Iguana Pattern

Ii

iguana

Ii

ink

ice

J Is for Jet

Materials

- CD or audio tape with a variety of music
- CD or tape player

Objective: Students will learn about music and the concept of speed.

Directions

1. Ask students about jets. Where do you see them? What do they do? Are they fast or slow?

2. Ask for examples of other things that are fast (cheetah, jaguar, rocket, horse, rabbit).

3. Ask for examples of things that are slow (turtle, donkey, syrup, penguin).

4. Play some slow music. Talk about the tempo. Play a sample of fast music. Talk about it.

5. Now play new music. Have students move to the beat of the music. Ask students if the music reminds them of a jet or a donkey.

6. Play music at a different tempo. Have students move to the beat of the music. Does this music remind them of a turtle or a rabbit?

J Is for Jar

Materials

- 1 copy of Jars, Jars, Jars! (page 74) for each child

- a variety of jars with contents (e.g., olives, pickles, beads)

Objective: Students will use listening skills to follow instructions.

Directions

1. Display jars with a variety of contents.

2. Have students guess which jar you are describing as you give a few oral clues.

3. Give each child a copy of Jars, Jars, Jars! Tell the students to listen carefully while you give directions to complete the sheet.

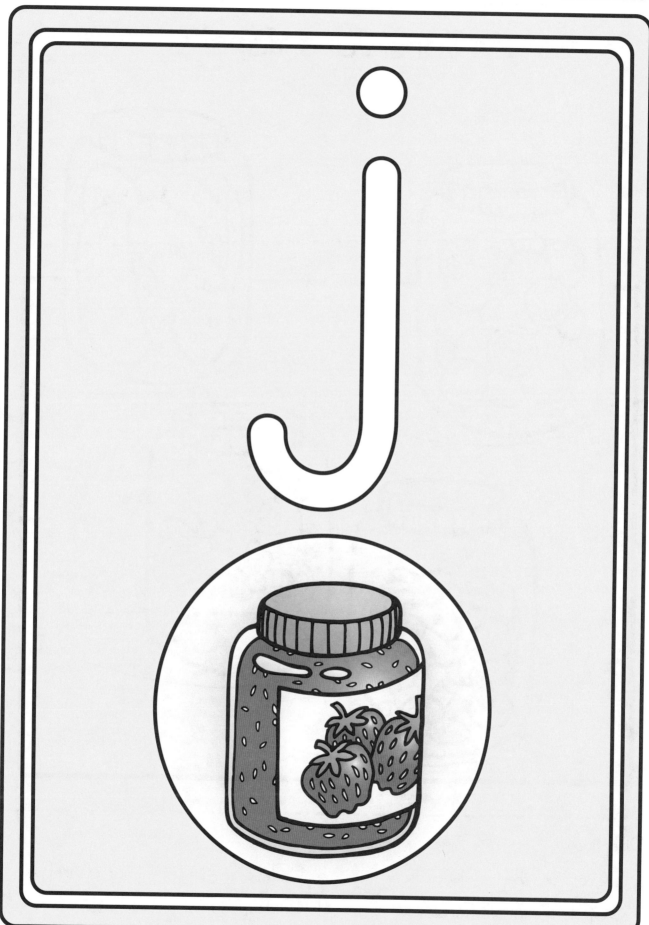

Name _____

Jars, Jars, Jars!

Directions

1. Cross out the jar of beads.

2. Circle the jar of marbles.

3. Draw a line under the jar of fireflies.

4. Color the jar of pickles green.

Jj

CIDER

jack-in-the-box

jug   jam

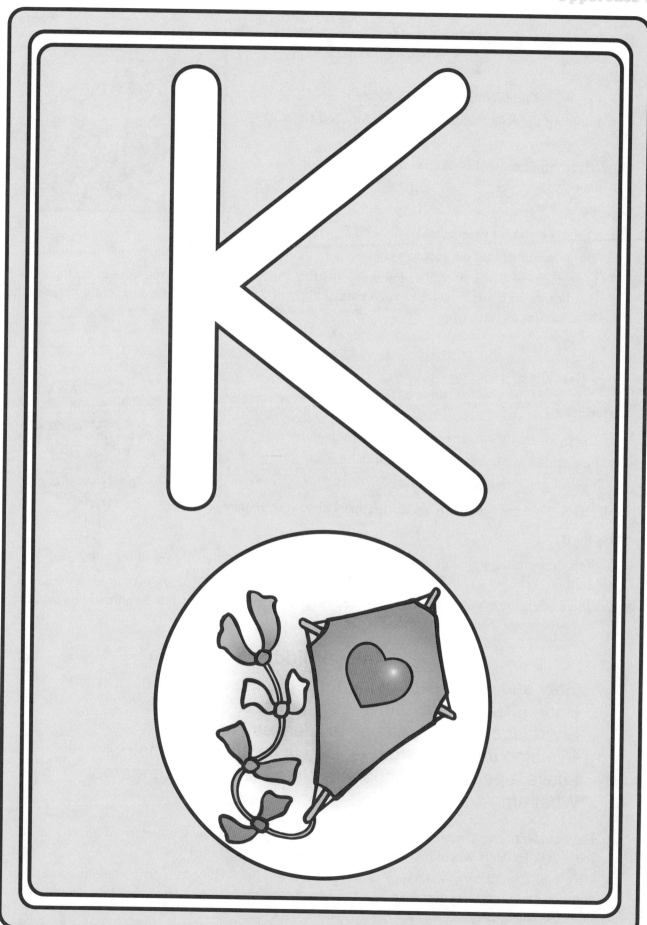

K Is for Kite

Materials

- 1 copy of Kite Pictures (page 80) for each child
- 1 copy of the Kite Patterns (page 81) for each child (1/2 page)

Objective: Students will review words that start with *k* in this activity.

Directions

1. Discuss different words that begin with *k*.
2. Have students point out pictures or objects in the room that begin with *k*.
3. Give each child a copy of Kite Patterns. Instruct him or her to color and cut out each picture that begins with a *k*. Then give each child a copy of Kite Pictures. Have the child paste each *k* picture on a kite.

K Is for Koala

Materials

- 1 copy of Koala Patterns (page 82) for each child
- picture of a koala and a joey in their habitat
- 1 small craft stick for each child

Objective: Students will learn interesting facts about the koala.

Directions

1. Tell the children a riddle. Explain that they need to listen carefully for clues: "I am an animal. I eat pet food. I wag my tail. What am I?" (*dog*)
2. Tell students you will give them another animal riddle. But this is not an animal you would have for a pet! Read aloud the riddle below.

Animal Riddle

Gray and white, ears of fur; I sleep a lot, and do not purr.
Round head, handy paws, long arms, strong claws.
Short legs, big feet, stubby tail, leaves I eat.
Climbing trees is my game, joey is my baby's name.
I have a pouch, just one more clue, I am **not** a kangaroo!
What am I?

3. Have students guess what animal the riddle is about. Then show the picture of a koala and a joey. Ask students where they might see koalas. (*zoo, Australia*)
4. Give each child a copy of Koala Patterns and a craft stick. Have him or her take it home, color and cut out the patterns, and glue the craft stick to the joey. Then the child can tell a family member about koalas using the koala and joey.

Kite Pictures

Directions: Glue each pattern from "Kite Patterns" that starts with *k* onto a kite.

Kite Patterns

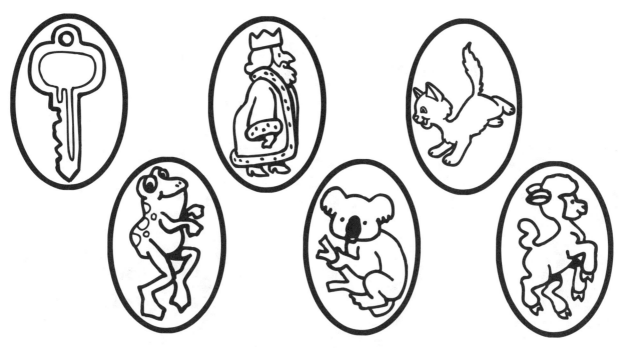

Directions: Color and cut out each picture that starts with *k*.
Glue the *k* pictures to the kites.

Kite Patterns

Directions: Color and cut out each picture that starts with *k*.
Glue the *k* pictures to the kites.

Koala Patterns

cut along pouch line

- -

Directions: Color and cut out the koala and joey patterns. Glue a craft stick to the back of the joey. Insert the joey in the koala's pocket and move it up and down to play hide-and-seek!

Kk

kite

Kk

kangaroo

king

L Is for Lion

Material

- yellow or orange hat

Objective: Students will reinforce oral language skills by playing action-packed game.

Directions

1. Explain to children that they will be playing a game called "Lion, Lion."

2. Have the child who is pretending to be the "lion" wear the hat. The other children will chant, "Lion, lion, you can't get me!"

3. The lion tries to tag a child. When the lion tags a child, he or she says, "Now I've got you and you can't go free."

4. The children that are captured are confined to a certain spot in the room until all of the children have been tagged.

L Is for Lamb

Materials

- 1 copy of Lovely Little Lambs (page 88) for each child
- 9 large cotton balls
- 9 small cotton balls for each child
- 1 small, resealable plastic bag for each child

Preparation: Place nine small cotton balls in a plastic bag for each child.

Objective: Students will practice one-to-one correspondence and addition with this take-home activity.

Directions

1. Tell students that you will be practicing counting and adding. Show them the large cotton balls. Have students pretend that each ball is a "lamb."

2. Have several volunteers show how to use the lambs to solve simple addition sentences (e.g., While five lambs were running, they met two more lambs. How many lambs in all?).

3. Send home a plastic bag filled with nine small cotton balls and a copy of Lovely Little Lambs. Explain to the children that they will glue one cotton ball on each lamb. Then, touch each lamb as they count the lambs on the first hill. The student writes the number of lambs in the first circle, with assistance if needed. Then he or she touches and counts the lambs on the second hill and writes the number in the second circle. Finally, the child touches each lamb while counting and writes the total number of lambs in the big box.

87

Lovely Little Lambs

Directions: Glue one cotton ball onto each lamb. Write the number of lambs on the first hill in the first circle. Write the number of lambs on the second hill in the second circle. Finally, touch each lamb while counting and write the total number of lambs in the square.

Ll

lion

Ll

lamb leaves

M Is for Me

Materials

- large poster board
- pointer

Preparation: Copy the "Me Poem" on a poster board to display for children.

Objective: Children will learn about different emotions while reciting this poem.

Directions

1. Read the "Me Poem" to the children several times. (Teacher Note: You may wish to substitute examples in the poem to address students' needs.)

2. Point to each word as the children repeat the poem with you.

3. Make a facial expression that corresponds with a line in the poem (i.e., a pouting, pretending to cry face for *Rainy days make me sad).* Have children guess which part of the poem you are demonstrating.

4. After you have demonstrated an expression for each line of the poem, slowly say the poem with the children while a different volunteer makes an expression for the corresponding line.

Me Poem

My birthdays make me happy,

Rainy days make me sad.

Loud noises make me scared,

Broken toys make me mad.

Scary stories make me surprised,

Good friends make me glad.

M Is for Mailbox

Materials

- 2 large boxes, 1 labeled "*m*," the other labeled "not *m*"
- objects to sort (some that begin with *m*)
- 1 copy of Mailbox Matching (page 94) for each child

Objective: Students will reinforce phonemic awareness skills with this sorting activity.

Directions

1. Talk about how letters are put in mailboxes, with the address on the envelope matching the words and numbers of the address on the house.

2. Have children help you sort objects into the two boxes: those that begin with *m* and those that do not begin with *m*.

3. Give each child a copy of Mailbox Matching. Have each child draw a line from each word that starts with *m* to a mailbox labeled with *M* or *m*.

Mailbox Matching

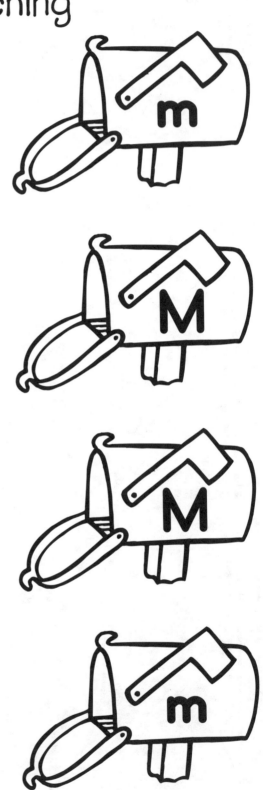

- -

Directions: Draw a line from each word that starts with *m* to a different mailbox.

Mm

moon Mm

monkey mouse

96

N is for Nose

Material

- a variety of distinct scents (e.g., apple juice, lemon juice, perfume, taco seasoning mix)
- several film canisters
- cotton balls

Preparation: Place a few cotton balls and sprinkle a distinct scent into each container. Label each one with a different numeral.

Objective: Students will use the sense of smell to distinguish different scents.

Directions

1. Talk about the nose and the sense of smell. Ask the children, "What kinds of things can you smell?" Use language associated with scent such as *sweet, strong,* and *spicy.*

2. Pass each canister around so that the children can smell each one.

3. Talk about scents the children liked or disliked, using the numbers marked on the canisters for proper identification. Have the children guess the different scents. Finally, identify each scent for the children.

N Is for Nest

Materials

- 1 egg carton
- 1 copy of Nest Graph (page 100) for each child

Preparation: Cut apart the egg carton into 12 cup-shaped sections. Title a graph, "Places We Have Seen Nests." Make a bar graph as shown on this page.

Objective: Students will practice graphing with this hands-on activity.

Directions

1. Show the children an egg carton section. Tell them that each one represents a nest.

2. Ask the children if they have seen nests at their homes, at the park, or at school. At a center, have each child put one "nest" on the graph to represent the nests he or she has seen at home, at a park, or at school.

3. Give each child a copy of Nest Graph to complete individually. Have each child count the nests for each person on the graph. The child writes the number of nests at the bottom of each column.

99

Name _____

Nest Graph

Kendra

Cora

Juan

I found ☐ nests in all.

Directions: Count the number of nests each child found. Write the number of nests *below* each name.

Nn

nest **Nn**

nine nuts

102

103

O Is for Octopus

Materials

- 1 white paper plate for every 2 children
- gray, white, pink, and peach crepe paper

Preparation: Cut each paper plate in half. Cut the crepe paper into equal-sized strips so that there are eight for each child.

Objective: Students will learn about the octopus *and* create an octopus to take home!

Directions

1. Talk about the octopus. Where does it live? (in the ocean) Tell the children that *oct* means eight. The octopus has eight tentacles. The tentacles are similar to our arms and legs.
2. Give each child half of a paper plate and eight crepe paper strips. Have each child count the strips to ensure that he or she has the correct number before beginning the project.
3. Instruct each child to make two eyes on the face of the octopus by drawing two black circles. Have him or her glue the crepe paper strips on the bottom of the plate for the legs.
4. Display the completed octopuses on a bulletin board with an ocean background. Title the display, "Observe Our Outrageous Octopuses!"

O Is for Ostrich

Materials

- 4 craft sticks for each child
- 1 enlarged copy of Ostrich Patterns (page 106) for the teacher
- 1 copy of Ostrich Patterns (page 106) for each child

Preparation: Use the enlarged copy to assemble one set of ostrich stick puppets.

Objective: In this oral language activity, children will share fun facts about the ostrich.

Directions

1. Show children the completed ostrich stick puppets. Ask children what they already know about the ostrich.
2. Remind children about the facts learned in "E Is for Egg" page 42. (The ostrich lays the largest egg; the hummingbird lays the smallest egg.)
3. Teach the children the words to the song, "A Special Bird." *(Note: Sing to the tune of the traditional song, "Row, Row, Row Your Boat.")*
4. Hold up each ostrich puppet during the corresponding line in the song. Have students complete the puppets as directed on "Ostrich Patterns" and use them while singing the song.
5. Have students practice telling facts about the ostrich, using the puppets and words from the song.

> ## A Special Bird
>
> Big, tall, brown ostrich,
> Runs with its long legs.
> Cannot fly into the air,
> But lays the largest eggs.

Ostrich Patterns

Directions: Color and cut out each picture. Glue each cutout onto a craft stick to create a stick puppet. Use the puppets to tell facts about the ostrich, using words from the song, "A Special Bird."

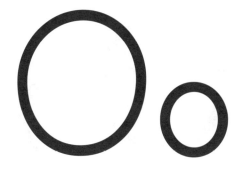

octopus Oo

otter   owl

P Is for Pizza

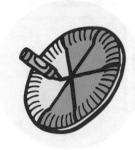

Materials

- 1 copy of Pizza Pieces (page 112) for each child
- 7 paper plates
- markers

Preparation: Divide each plate into six "slices" of pizza. Color in different fractions on the plates. Color one whole pizza.

Objective: Students will learn about *more* and *less* with this simple fraction activity.

Directions

1. Show the completely colored plate. Describe it as a whole pizza, with no missing pieces.
2. Then show a plate that has half of the pizza (3 slices) colored in. Ask, "Which pizza has more slices left to eat?"
3. Give each child a copy of the Pizza Pieces worksheet. Explain to the children that they should carefully look at each row to see which of the pizzas has fewer slices left. Have children cross out the pizza in each row that has fewer slices.

P Is for Pig

Materials

- none

Objective: Reinforce counting skills with this action-packed song.

Directions

1. Teach students "The Pigs Go Skipping" song. *(Note: Sing to the tune of the traditional song, "Ants Go Marching.")*
2. Have the children sing the song with one child performing the action for the first verse, two children for the second verse, etc. Repeat until all have had a chance to participate.

The Pigs Go Skipping

The pigs go skipping one by one,
oh yes, oh yes!
The pigs go skipping one by one,
oh yes, oh yes!
The pigs go skipping one by one,
The little one stops to beat his drum,
Chorus
And they all go skipping down to the ground,
To get out of the pen!
Boom! Boom! Boom!

The pigs go galloping two by two,
oh yes, oh yes . . .
The little one stops to tie his shoe,
Chorus
The pigs go hopping three by three,
oh yes, oh yes . . .
The little one stops to climb a tree,
Chorus
The pigs go running four by four,
oh yes, oh yes . . .
The little one stops to shut the door,
Chorus

Name _____

Pizza Pieces

Directions: Look at the pizzas in each row. Cross out the pizza that has fewer pieces in each row.

Pp

pigs   Pp

pizza   peach

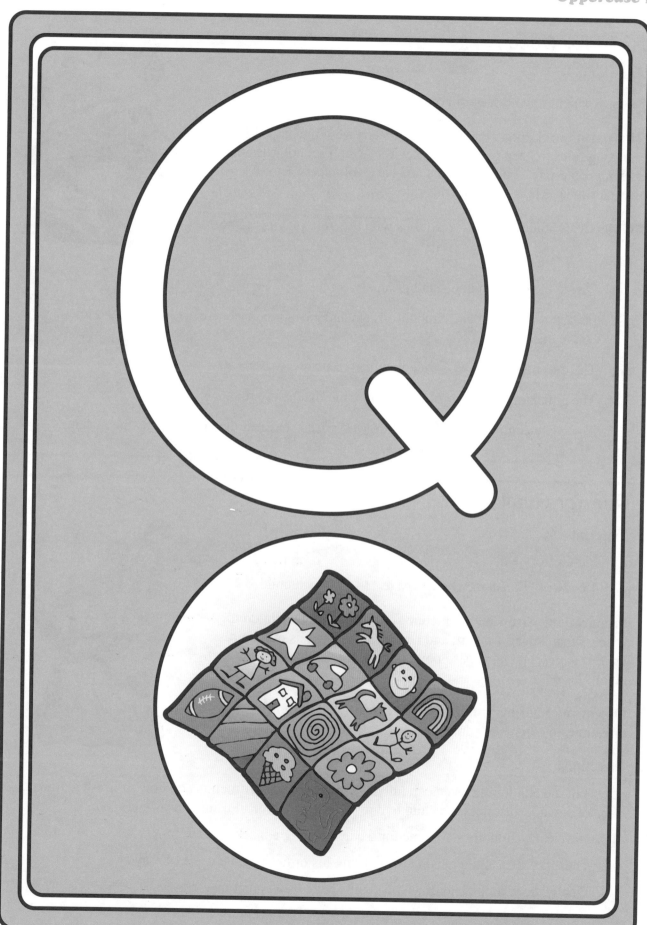

Q Is for Queen

Materials

- 1 paper crown (for each group)

Preparation: Explain that long ago, queens were in charge of making rules to keep people safe. Review several school rules that keep people safe. Select one rule and have volunteers act out a scene showing how to follow this rule.

Objective: Students will review rules with this role-playing game.

Directions

1. Divide the children into small groups.

2. In each group, give one child the crown and have him or her wear it and pretend to be the queen.

3. The queen shares a safety rule with the group.

4. The remaining children role-play following that safety rule.

5. The game continues until each child who wishes has had the chance to be the queen.

Q Is for Quail

Materials

- Pictures of quails
- 1 copy of "Finish the Quail" (page 118) for each child

Preparation: Share several pictures of quails with the children. Discuss that a quail is a bird and has the same parts as other birds: *a beak*, *wings*, and *feet*. Also point out the *plume* on top of the quail's head.

Objective: Students will learn about a quail while following directions to complete a drawing.

Directions

1. Tell the children to listen carefully as you give them instructions on how to finish a drawing of a quail. Instruct each child to draw a foot on the quail using a brown crayon.

2. Have each child draw a plume for the quail using a black crayon.

3. Then direct the child to add a wing using his or her favorite color of crayon.

4. Finally, have each child draw the quail's beak using an orange crayon.

Name _____

Finish the Quail

Directions

1. Draw a *foot* using a brown crayon.

2. Draw a *plume* using a black crayon.

3. Draw a *wing* using the crayon of your choice.

4. Draw a *beak* using an orange crayon.

Qq

quilt   Qq

quail queen

R Is for Rain

Materials

- books about rainy days (*In the Rain with Baby Duck* by Amy Hest, *Listen to the Rain* by Bill Martin Jr. and John Archambault)
- chart paper
- light blue construction paper
- marker

Preparation: Cut out raindrop shapes from the blue construction paper.

Objective: Students will sharpen listening skills and create a class story.

Directions

1. Share books about rain with the children

2. Have children list words that appeared in more than one book (*rain, cloud, cloudy, wet, puddle, muddy, raincoat, soaked*).

3. Write each word on a raindrop cutout.

4. Have students use the words on the raindrops to create a class story about a rainy day. (Students dictate the sentences while the teacher writes them on the chart.) Attach each raindrop to the correct place in the story as the word is used.

R Is for Rabbit

Materials

- 1 copy of Rabbit Stories (page 124) for each child

Objective: Students will create a story based on a picture.

Directions

1. Talk about rabbits. What do they do? What do they eat? Where do they live?

2. Give each child a copy of Rabbit Stories. Model how to use the worksheet to tell a story. Choose a scene from the worksheet and then tell a short story about the scene.

3. Have each child choose his or her favorite scene and color it.

4. Divide the class into pairs. Have each student tell his or her partner a story based on his or her favorite scene.

5. Students can take the sheet home to share with their families.

Name _____

Rabbit Stories

Directions: Choose your favorite scene and color it. Tell your partner a story about the scene.

Rr

rhinoceros **Rr**

ram rabbit

S Is for Sunflower

Materials

- 1 paper plate for each child
- orange and yellow colored paper
- sunflower seeds

Preparation: Cut the colored paper into small triangles.

Objective: Students will create a sunflower in this "sun"-sational, textured art project!

Directions

1. Ask students, "Have you ever seen a sunflower? What color was it? Was it big or small? What did the flower part look like?"

2. Tell students that they will be making their own sunflowers. Give each child a paper plate, paper triangles, and sunflower seeds. Instruct them to glue the triangles around the plate to create petals for the sunflower. Have students glue seeds in the middle of the plate.

3. Display the sunflowers on a bulletin board titled "See Our Sun–sational Sunflowers!"

S Is for Sock

Materials

- pairs of shoes
- pairs of socks
- 1 copy of Sorting Socks (page 130) for each child
- 4 large paper clips for each child
- clothespins

Objective: Children will sort shoes and socks into matching pairs.

Directions

1. Demonstrate how to sort shoes and socks to find pairs. Emphasize looking for patterns, sizes, and colors on the socks to correctly make pairs.

2. Have volunteers create pairs by sorting the remaining shoes and socks.

3. Place the socks at a Sorting Center. Have children match the pairs. Then, have them clip each pair together using a clothespin.

4. Give each child a copy of Sorting Socks and four paper clips. Have them color and cut out the socks. Then, have them sort the socks into pairs. Use paper clips to attach each pair together.

Sorting Socks

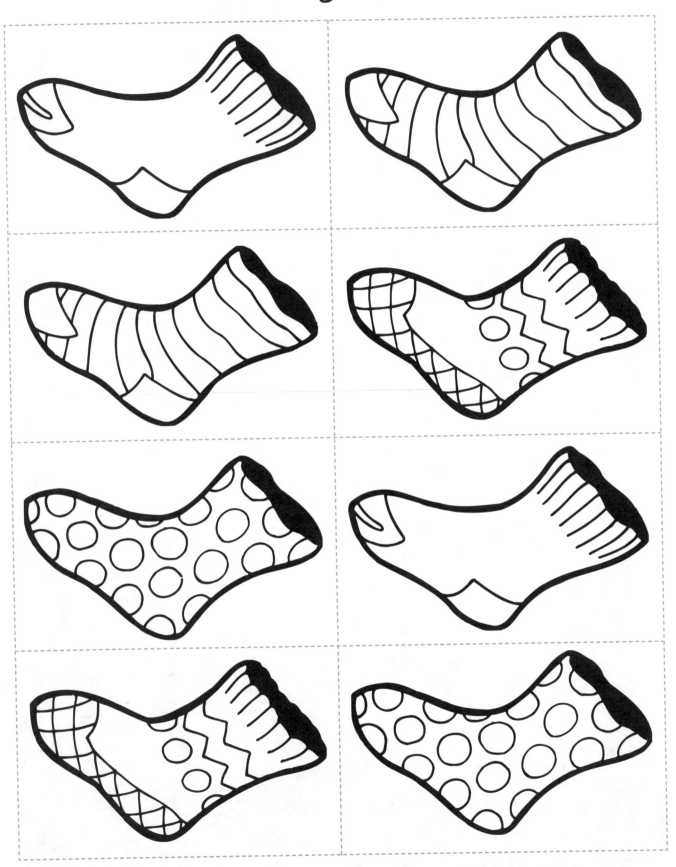

Directions: Color and cut out the socks. Sort the socks into pairs.

Ss

sandwich   Ss

snake skunk

T Is for Teeth

Materials

- toothbrush
- dental floss
- toothpaste
- egg carton cut in half, lengthwise

Objective: Students will learn how to properly care for their teeth during this activity.

Directions

1. Talk about teeth and how to take care of them. Show students the toothbrush, floss, and toothpaste. Have the students explain how each item helps keep their teeth clean. Demonstrate how to floss, using the egg carton strip as a row of teeth.

2. Ask students if they have had a chance to visit the dentist. Allow volunteers to share good things about their visits.

3. Review foods that are good for teeth (e.g., milk, vegetables, fruit, cheese) and bad for teeth (e.g., candy, cookies, cake). Remind the children that they should try to eat a variety of things that are good for teeth and only a small amount of things that are not.

T Is for Tiger

Materials

- 1 copy of "T"-rrific Tiger (page 136) for each child
- chart
- marker

Objective: Students will identify nouns that begin with the letter *t*.

Directions

1. Talk about tigers, the largest wild cats in the world. Where do they live? (*Asia*) What do they eat? (*other animals*)

2. Ask volunteers to share with the class words that begin with *t*. List the words on a chart.

3. Give each child a copy of "T"-rrific Tiger. Tell the children they will complete a story by inserting a picture in the correct place. Remind students that they are studying the letter *t*, and that each picture in this story about a tiger will also begin with *t*.

4. Invite volunteers to share what they think each picture represents on the activity sheet. Have each student take the sheet home and complete it by following the written directions.

"T"-rrific Tiger

A baby [   ] is called a cub.

It can climb a [   ] .

It has claws and [   ] .

Cubs stay with their mothers until they are [   ] .

- -

Directions: Cut out the *t* pictures at the bottom. As a family member reads each sentence, attach the corresponding picture to the appropriate place.

T t

turtle   Tt

tricycle   teapot

U Is for Umbrella

Materials

- 1 Styrofoam® plate for each child

- 1 candy cane for each child

- markers

Objective: Students will create an umbrella to get in the mood for a rainy day!

Directions

1. Tell the children that they will be making umbrellas. Give each child a plate and access to markers. Allow time to draw special designs on the plates.

2. Have each child complete his or her umbrella by inserting the stick of the candy cane into the middle of the plate.

3. Remind students of the lyrics to "Rain, Rain." (*Rain, rain, go away/Come again some other day!*) Repeat the verse a few times.

4. Have the children carry their umbrellas over their heads while singing "Rain, Rain," pretending they are outside on a very rainy day!

U Is for Unicorn

Materials

- 1 copy of Unicorn Search (page 142) for each child

- unicorn stuffed animal or an illustration of a unicorn

Objective: Children will practice one-to-one correspondence with this whimsical activity.

Directions

1. Talk about unicorns. Tell children that *uni* means one and *unicorn* means "one horn."

2. Show the unicorn stuffed animal or picture of a unicorn. Share with students that *unicycle* means "one wheel." Ask students if they have ever seen someone ride a unicycle at a circus or other event.

3. Give each child a copy of Unicorn Search. Have them find each unicorn and circle it. Remind students that true unicorns have only one horn!

Name _____

Unicorn Search

Directions: Color each unicorn that has one horn.

U u

unicorn Uu

umbrella unicycle

V Is for Vest

Materials

- vest with a pattern or scene on it
- 1 copy of Very Cool Vests (page 148) for each child

Objective: Students will practice matching skills with this hands-on activity.

Directions

1. Show the students a vest. Describe how each side of the vest matches, or how a scene is continued on both sides.

2. Talk about how vests usually have two halves; one on the right side and the other on the left. Ask children if they think the pattern should be the same on both halves of the vest.

3. Give each child a copy of Very Cool Vests. Have them cut out the vest halves at the bottom of the page and glue the halves on the corresponding vests.

V Is for Violin

Materials

- violin or picture of a violin
- CD or cassette tape of violin music
- CD or cassette player

Preparation: Select violin music that is very loud or soft at times; and very fast or slow at times.

Objective: Students will review the concepts of the opposites *loud/soft* and *fast/slow*.

Directions

1. Show the students the violin or picture of a violin. Ask them questions about it. (*Is it a musical instrument? What types of sounds does it make? How does it work?*)

2. Have students listen to violin music. Ask them if they heard parts that were loud. Did they hear parts that were slow? fast? soft?

3. Allow the children to share with the class how the music made them feel.

Name _____

Very Cool Vests

Directions: Cut out the vest parts at the bottom of the page. Glue each half onto the corresponding vest.

valentine

Vv

violin   vegetables

W Is for Web

Materials

- ball of yarn

Preparation: Explain that kindness and getting along with others can go a long way. Give examples of compliments.

Objective: Students will use this web of friendship to practice thinking of and giving compliments.

Directions

1. Gather the children in a circle on the floor.

2. A child starts the web by rolling the ball of yarn to a teacher.

3. The teacher gives a compliment to the child (the person who rolled the yarn to him or her), holds the ball of yarn, and rolls it to another child.

4. Repeat in the same manner until all the children have received a compliment.

5. The last child rolls the yarn back to the teacher, who then gives him or her a compliment.

6. Have the children look at the beautiful web of friendship they have created!

W Is for Water

Materials

- water table filled with water
- shallow container
- assortment of land animal and water animal toys
- 1 copy of What Lives in the Water? for each child

Preparation: Explain to the children that some animals live on land (e.g., tigers, monkeys, raccoons). Then tell them that some animals live in the water. Have the children brainstorm a list of several water animals. Give students the What Lives in the Water? activity to complete with an adult at home.

Objective: Students will sort animals into two groups based on where the animals live.

Directions

1. Look carefully at all the animal toys in the water table.

2. Separate the toy animals into two groups: land animals and water animals.

3. Take out the land animals, leaving the water animals in the water table. Discuss the choices.

Name _____

What Lives in the Water?

Directions: Color each animal that lives in water. Cross out each animal that lives only on land.

Ww

witches Ww

whale watermelon

X Is for Bo<u>x</u>

Materials

- boxes with lids in a variety of sizes and shapes (e.g., ring box, shirt box, copy paper box, gift box)
- 1 copy of Boxes of Fun (page 160) for each child

Preparation: Display a variety of boxes separate from their lids.

Objective: Students will practice shape recognition with this math activity.

Directions

1. Ask students how boxes are used. Have them give some examples (e.g., shoes, toys, cereal, storage, moving).
2. Have student volunteers match each box with its corresponding lid.
3. Discuss the different shapes and sizes.
4. Give each child a copy of Boxes of Fun. Have a volunteer show how to match the first lid with its corresponding box. Instruct students to complete the activity independently.

X Is for X-ray

Materials

- 1 copy of X-ray Pattern (page 161) for each child
- 1 copy of Squirrel Patterns (page 162) for each child
- 1 cereal box (11" tall [28 cm]) for each child
- black paper
- tape
- clear cellophane

Preparation: On the front of each box, cut out a large rectangular shape. Leave a border.

Objective: Students will build their own x-ray machines.

Directions

1. Cover the outside of the box with black paper.
2. Give each child a copy of X-ray Pattern page and the Squirrel Patterns page. Have them color and cut out the patterns.
3. Glue the skeleton inside the box.
4. Tape a piece of cellophane inside the box. (This will be the window of the x-ray machine.)
5. Glue the head (Tab A) to the top of the back of the box.
6. Glue the arms (Tab B) to the back edges of the box.
7. Glue the feet (Tab C) to the bottom back of the box.

159 #8008 Alphabet: Cards, Activities, and Games

Boxes of Fun

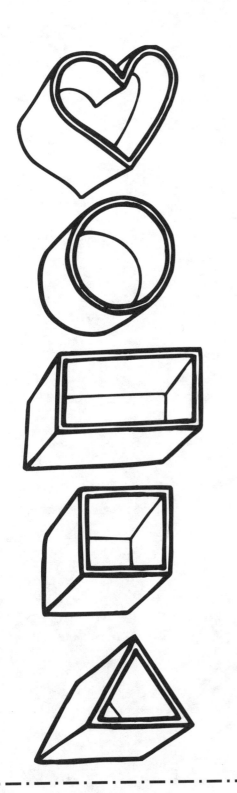
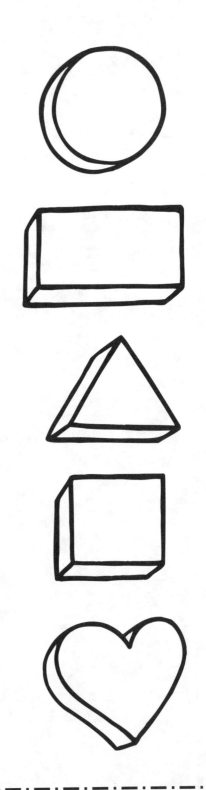

Directions: Draw a line from each box to its corresponding lid.

X-ray Pattern

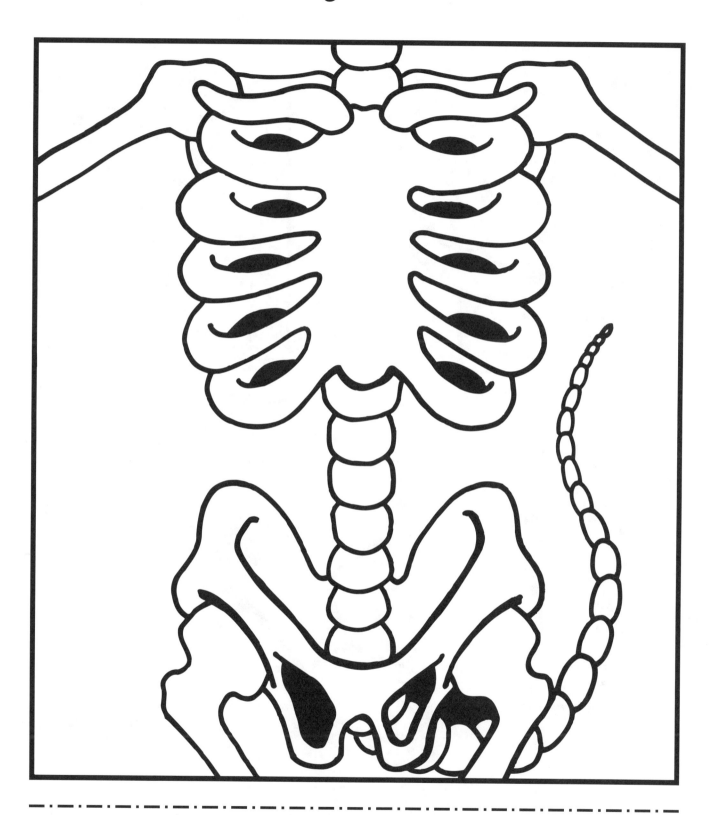

Directions: Use this page with page 162. Cut out the patterns and assemble them as directed by your teacher.

Squirrel Patterns

Tab A

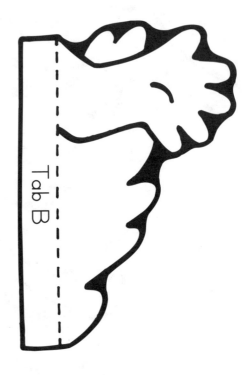

Tab B

Tab B

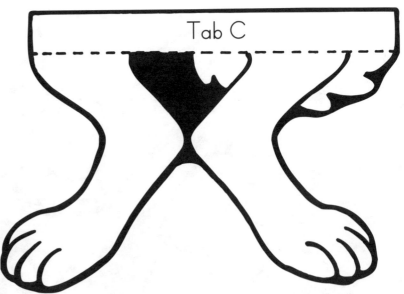

Tab C

Directions: Color and cut out the patterns. Assemble them as directed by your teacher.

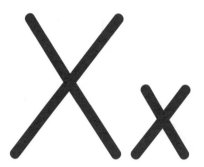

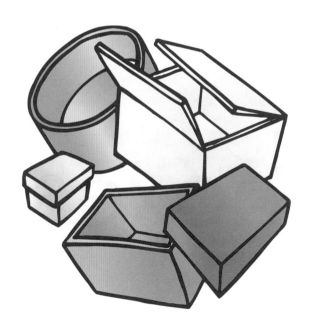

x-ray Xx

boxes fox

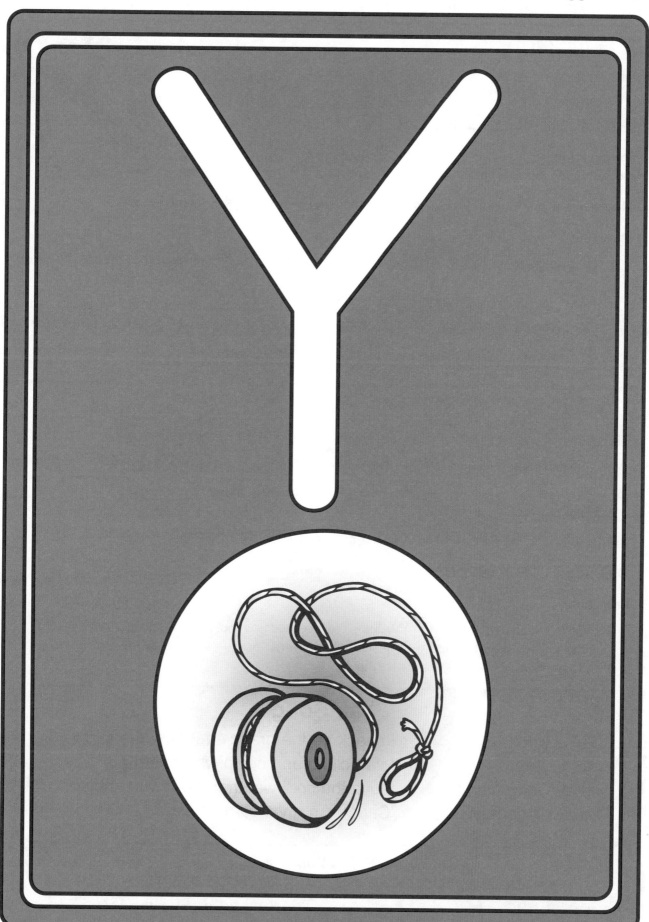

Y Is for Yarn

Materials

- yarn
- 1 sheet of paper for each child

Preparation: Cut part of the yarn into as many strips as you have students. In addition, cut three pieces of yarn (one very long, two shorter).

Objective: Children will practice forming the letter *y* by doing this tactile activity.

Directions

1. Have three volunteers show the class how to make a huge *Y* with the three additional pieces of precut yarn.

2. Give each child a sheet of paper and a strip of yarn. Have him or her cut the strip into two pieces (one long and one short). Then the child forms the letter *y* by gluing the strips on the paper.

Y Is for Yak

Materials

- cardstock paper
- string
- paper puncher

Preparation: Copy the Yak Mask (page 168) onto heavy cardstock paper.

Objective: Students will pretend to be yaks while singing about their characteristics!

Directions

1. Teach students the words to "Yak Song." Have students repeat each line after you several times. Then sing the song with the children. (*Note: Sing to the tune of the traditional song, "Three Blind Mice"*)

Yak Song

I'm a yak,	I snack on the grass and drink the snow,
I'm a yak.	I can climb and climb wherever I go.
I have long hair,	I love the cold weather, don't you know!
I have long hair.	'Cause I'm a yak, I'm a yak.

---

2. Give each child a copy of Yak Mask. Have him or her cut it out, help him or her punch holes as indicated, and attach string to the sides. Don't forget to cut holes for eyes.

3. Encourage the children to wear their yak masks as they sing the "Yak Song."

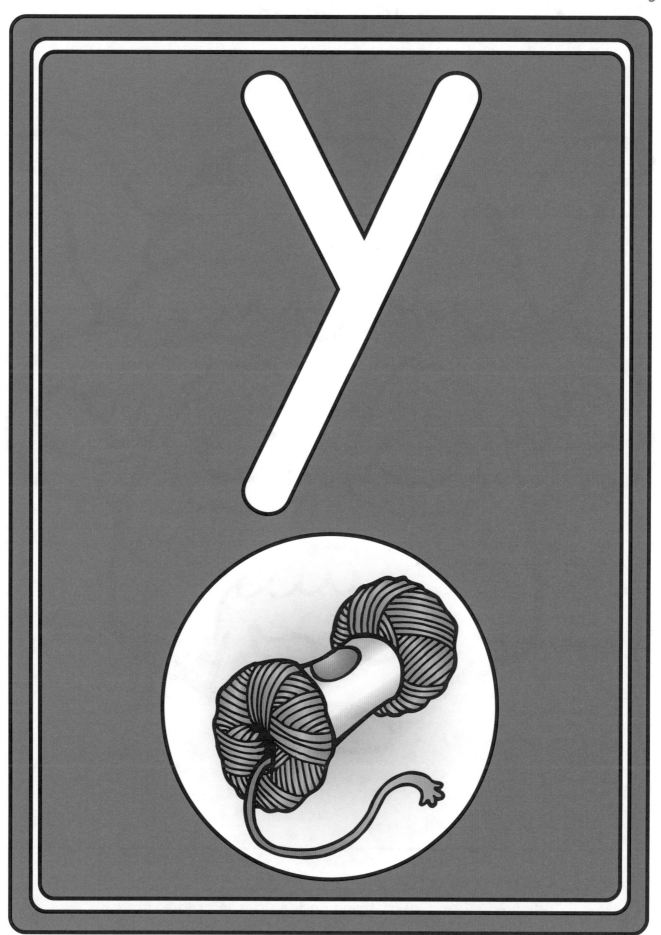

Yak Mask

Directions: Color and cut out the yak. Cut holes for eyes. Punch holes where indicated ⊗ and insert string on the sides to create a mask.

Y y

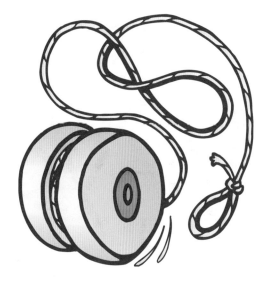

yo-yo   Y y

yak   yarn

Z Is for Zebra

Materials

- chart paper
- marker
- pointer

Preparation: Write the tongue twister on chart paper.

Objective: Students will repeat a tongue twister and identify the /z/ sound.

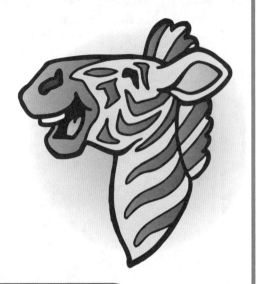

Directions

1. Teach students the following tongue twister:

> Zany Zora Zebra zips and zigzags at the zoo.

2. While you point to each *z* word, have students say the word and exaggerate the /z/ sound.

3. Repeat the tongue twister and have the children write the letter *z* in the air for each *z* word.

4. Challenge students to say the tongue twister as quickly as possible!

Z Is for Zoo

Materials

- 1 copy of Zoo Animals (page 174) for each child

Objective: Students will review the differences between zoo animals and pets with this fun activity sheet.

Directions

1. Ask students, "What animals have you seen at the zoo? What types of animals are your favorites? Why are the animals in cages?"

2. Then ask students about the types of animals they have for pets, or pets they would like to have.

3. Talk about the differences between animals that live at the zoo and animals that can live in your home (e.g., safety issues, animals' exotic needs).

4. Have each child complete Zoo Animals by cutting out only the zoo animals and gluing them in their cages.

Name _____

Zoo Animals

- -

Directions: Cut out each zoo animal and glue it in a cage.

Z z

zoo

Zz

zipper zebra